Discover your

Ancestors

Researching & Locating Your Ancestors

Celia Heritage

Discover Your Ancestors
Researching & Locating Your Ancestors

First published in 2015
Discover Your Ancestors Publishing
www.discoveryourancestors.co.uk

Printed and bound in Great Britain by Acorn Web Offset, Wakefield

A catalogue record for this book is available from the British Library

ISBN 978-1-911166-00-9

Written by Celia Heritage
Edited by Andrew Chapman

Design: Prepare to Publish Ltd

Contents

Part Three: Taking things further

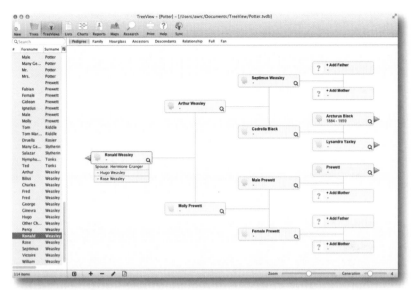

Treeview from TheGenealogist is an excellent way to keep track of your family tree research

Displaying and storing your family tree

As your family tree grows, you will need a means of storing all your information and of drawing a family tree. You may also wish to share and exchange information with other people. The Tree View app at TheGenealogist is an ideal tool which you can use on any PC, Mac or mobile device and, once it is uploaded, is not reliant on internet access to work. You can edit your tree from any device and it will be updated on any other device the next time it is turned on. Either add your information directly to the app or import it from another family tree program. Make sure you use the 'Source' feature' to verify the information on your tree as you go, while you can add notes to your tree and swap between displaying your tree in a variety of different styles of chart.

Part Two

Core records back to Victorian times

Befefore the advent of the internet, researchers had limited options as to where they could access sources and most of us had to travel to look at the sources we needed. Nowadays there is a wealth of information available to you online. The downside is that there is so much information out there many people are unsure as to where to start their search or they use unreliable sources. In some cases they end up tracing a family tree which is not actually theirs because of this. It is important to know which record sets or sources you should be searching and where to find them, rather than irrationally gleaning any information you can which seems to relate to an ancestor from online sources.

Your two core sources to take your family tree back to the start of Victorian times (1837) are:

- Records of civil registration, ie birth, marriage and death certificates
- Census returns.

You should use these two sets of records in tandem, as the information they supply complements each other and will make searching easier and more accurate. For example, finding an ancestor on the census returns will tell you his age (indicating his approximate year of birth) and his place of birth. This will make it easier to locate the correct birth certificate. Once you have his birth certificate this will tell you not just his parents' names, but also his mother's maiden name – something you will not find in the census records. Checking details in both sets of records is also another way of double checking you have found the right person. It's easy to order the wrong certificate for someone, especially if the surname is a common one. It's important to understand the origins of each record set and how the information in them was collected too; this will help you spot any errors in the records.

Before we go on to look at census and civil registration records in detail, here are a few points to consider about the way in which we search and our expectations.

General problems with searching

One thing that makes a good researcher is the ability to 'think outside the box' and not be constrained by our expectations. This especially applies when we are searching for our ancestors online in birth, marriage and death (BMD) records or census returns and we fail to find what we are looking at. Follow these rules which you will find helpful:

EARLIER POPULATION LISTINGS

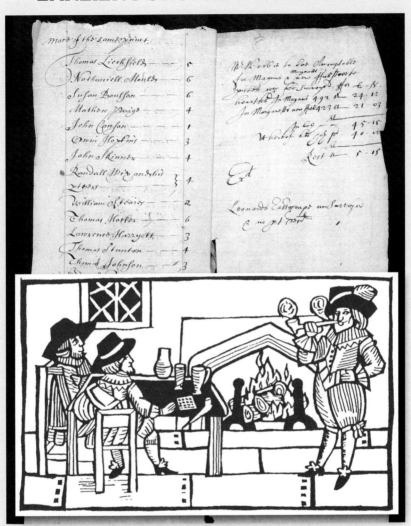

For earlier research there were many lists created as a result of taxes levied by the government, eg poll tax, hearth tax, window tax. The listings rarely include all the population (frequently omitting the poor and women) but are a useful tool for tracing surname distribution and may give you clues as to where to target your searches in other sources if you have lost an ancestor. These sources may also give you an idea of your ancestor's financial status depending on how much tax they paid. Land tax, which was collected between 1693 and 1963, is particularly useful in this respect, while transcriptions of hearth tax records (levied 1660-1689 – example above) are available for free for several counties at **www.hearthtax.org.uk**. For more on early tax listings look at TNA's research guide entitled 'Taxation before 1689'.

TRADE DIRECTORIES

Trade directories offer a wealth of information for family and local history. The pages here, from Kelly's 1877 directory for Buckinghamshire and Oxfordshire and available at **www.TheGenealogist.co.uk**, show, for example:

• Interesting advertisements, which may even include your ancestor's business

• Information about the history of towns and villages in the region

• Other useful details of local institutions, such as churches and workhouses

• Place-based (street-by-street for larger towns and cities) listings of people and their occupations.

OXFORDSHIRE.

OXFORDSHIRE, sometimes called Oxon, is an inland shire; it lies along the north shore of the Thames, the windings of which it follows, and it is, therefore, very irregular in shape, being in some places only 7 miles across, and in others, as in the north-west, 28; its greatest length is about 50 miles; it runs in a north-west and south-east direction, having its longest dimensions on the river side; it contains 752 square miles, or about 470,095 acres, and had a population in 1851 of 170,439; in 1861 of 170,944; and in 1871, 177,975, viz., males, 87,466; females, 90,509: it is bounded on the north by Warwickshire and by the river Cherwell and Northamptonshire,—on the east by Buckinghamshire,—on the south by the Thames and Berkshire,—and on the west by Gloucestershire; it is a country having a very varied surface, from the lowlands of the river to high and bare chalk hills: it belongs partly to the secondary formations and partly to the chalk, and is traversed by the Chiltern Hills from south-east to north-east, and by other ranges. The soil on the river bank is a rich black mould,—in north Oxfordshire it is a very fertile red earth or clay,—in the midland district it is a decomposed stonebrash or limestone, with sand and loam,—and in the Chilterns, or south-east, it is a sandy loam laid on the chalk. The rivers are numerous, and mostly belong to the basin of the Thames, which is the chief waterway: this river is popularly called the Thames throughout its course, but is properly the Isis until after the junction of the Thame; it enters the county at Lechlade, being navigable for vessels of ninety tons; its winding course forms the boundary of the county down to Henley. The Thame flows from Buckinghamshire past Thame and crosses Oxfordshire, past Dorchester, to its junction with the Isis between Day's lock and Shillingford bridge: after this junction the Isis is properly called the Thames. The Windrush rises in Gloucestershire, and in the Cotswold Hills, passes Burford and Witney, to the Isis. The Cherwell comes from Northamptonshire, enters Oxfordshire in the north near Claydon, and runs to the Isis near Oxford. The Evenlode rises in Worcestershire and, after receiving the Glyme near Woodstock, falls into the Isis about 4 miles above Oxford. The river Ray falls into the Cherwell. The Oxford canal enters the county at Banbury, and passes by the Cherwell to Oxford; it was begun in 1790, and is 91 miles long. By the Thames and the canals, Oxfordshire has water communication to every part of England.

The chief railway is the Great Western, which does not, however, enter the shire, but follows the other bank of the Thames; it sends off branches from Didcot to Oxford, and from Twyford by Shiplake to Henley. From Oxford are lines in connection with the Great Western to Chipping Norton, Evesham, Worcester, Droitwich, Kidderminster, Dudley and Wolverhampton; to Warwick and Birmingham, passing Woodstock and Banbury; from Oxford also are branches to Thame, Princes Risborough, Aylesbury and Winslow, joining the North Western at the latter place, and the main line of the Great Western at Taplow. A line is

being constructed in the north-west from Banbury to Cheltenham, utilising the present Chipping Norton branch.

The East Gloucestershire railway extends from Oxford through Witney to Lechlade and Fairford, Gloucestershire, and the company have power to continue it to Cheltenham, taking in its route the fertile agricultural district of the Colne Valley; the Act also empowers the company to construct a branch line from Lechlade to Faringdon.

The London and North Western Railway has a line from Bletchley, through [...] on this line, is a bra[...] to Banbury.

From Watlington [...] borough by the Watl[...] Company.

The county is con[...] system of railways [...] and South Eastern [...] The climate of Ox[...] than other southern [...] considered favourab[...] raised of wheat, be[...] beans, carrots, potat[...] purposes. In the r[...] river and streams ca[...] the hills are wood[...] sent down the river[...] hogs are also bred [...] coarse building ston[...] pottery), lime, slate [...] manufactures are bl[...] weaving and agricul[...] at Banbury; and g[...] tweeds are made a[...] mills on the banks [...] country women. C[...] to some extent, prin[...] near Tetsworth.

Oxfordshire is in [...] of Canterbury, dioc[...] shire town is Oxford [...] twelve market town[...] has one court of q[...] divisions.

The county of Ox[...] the city of Oxford [...] two; Woodstock se[...] Oxford is a well-built city on the Thames, with a population in 1871 of 34,482; it is remarkable for its University, and is also the see of a bishop. Witney, Woodstock and Banbury are small manufacturing towns. Woodstock has near it the palace of Blenheim, the seat of the Duke of Marlborough. Thame, Henley (famed for its regatta), Deddington, Chipping Norton, Watlington, Bicester, Bampton and Burford are market towns. Dorchester, also a market town,

64*

DIRECTORY.] **OXFORDSHIRE.** KIDLINGTON. 1017

KIDDINGTON is a parish consisting of the hamlets of NETHER KIDDINGTON in Wootton hundred, and OVER KIDDINGTON in Chadlington hundred. They are pleasantly situated on the river Glyme, which separates them, 67 miles from London, about 4 north from Woodstock, 6 from Heyford railway station and from Charlbury station, in Woodstock union and county court district, rural deanery of Woodstock and archdeaconry and diocese of Oxford. The church of St. Nicholas is an ancient structure in good repair, consisting of chancel, nave, south transept and west tower with bells; there is an ancient brass to the memory of the Walter Goodyear; a handsome stained window has been placed in the transept to the memory of Mrs. G... who died 27th December, 1872. The register date the year 1553. The living is a rectory, yearly £497, in the gift of Viscount Dillon and held Rev. John Geoffry Browne, M.A. of Trinity C

Nether Kiddington.

BrowneRev.JohnGeoffry,M.A.[rector], Radford Jo
Rectory
Gaskell Henry Lomax, esq. J.P., D.L. Busby Geo
Kiddington hall Fifield Sa
Radford George, farmer Hunt Geo

KIDLINGTON is a large village and paris the parliamentary borough of Woodstock, sit the Cherwell, in the hundred of Wootton, W union and county court district, rural deanery stock and archdeaconry and diocese of Oxford from London, 5 north from Oxford and 4 from Woodstock. The Woodstock Road stati Great Western railway is in this parish, thre of a mile distant from the village; there is als at Kirtlington, 2 miles distant, also on the G ern railway. The Oxford canal passes th parish. The church of St. Mary is a very sp beautiful cruciform edifice with a square mounted by a slender spire; it is in the Ea and Norman styles; there is a fine stain above the communion table, by the side o some old oak pews, curiously carved, and ano window at the west end, erected in 1858 to of the late vicar, Joseph Loscombe Richard register dates from the year 1630. The livi age with Water Eaton annexed, joint yearl with residence, annexed to the rectorshi College, Oxford; the Rev. John Pridea D.D. Rector of Exeter College, is the incu is a National school. The Wesleyans have An hospital was erected in 1671 by Sir Wil Chief Justice of the Common Pleas, in u

Kidlington.

Bathe Richard, Hampden villa
Bellow Rev. William, M.A. [curate],The
Vicarage
Borton Matthew
Braine Mrs
Braine William
Butler Mrs
Dixon Mrs
Gibbs William
Forster Mrs
Hastings Mrs
Hutt Frederick
Hutt Miss
Nowers Rev. James Edward Laurence,
B.A. [curate], The Vicarage
Parry Henry Hitchcock
Preedy Joseph
Rogers Mrs
Rouse John Wild
Rowland Joseph, Thornbury house
Simmonds Misses
Smith Mrs
Stapleton Bryan J. Grove house
Ward Mrs
Wilkinson William
Adams Alfred, grocer & agent for W.
& A. Gilbey, wine & spirit merchants
Bateman John, baker
... William, grocer

Dublin. A National school was built and is supported by H. L. Gaskell, esq. Kiddington Hall, the seat of Henry Lomax Gaskell, esq. D.L. who is lord of the manor and principal landowner, is a handsome and ... residence, surrounded by lawns and park, ... The soil is stone

Clarke...
Clarke William, *Anchor*
Collins James, grocer
Cummins Ellen (Miss), school
Harris James, farmer
Heath William, *Six Bells*
Hill John, carpenter
Hill Thomas, wheelwright
Honor Joseph, painter
Warland Henry, ...
Watts Thomas, cowkeeper
Woodford George, farmer
Wren Thomas, blacksmith
Wren John, carpenter
Young Richard, *Dog & Anchor*

52

	1702	1705		1702	1705
John Smith	M	St	William Philips ...... S St	I	C
William Collis	M	I	William Linnel ...... S St	I	C
			Samuel Rose .... I C	I	C
UPTON.			Richard Freeman .... I C	I	C
Major Fairchild	I	C	Jonathan Newbold.... I C	I	C
			Thomas Carre........ S	I	C
WHILTON.			Richard Grandborow.. S St	M	I
John Emery	S	I	Robert Carre .... S	I	C
Thomas Westley	S	St	John Dunckly	M	St
William Collins	S	St	John Billingham......	M	St
John Curtis..........	I	C	Thomas Mutton	St	C
William Sharman	I	C	William Butlin	I	C
Daniel Rowe	S	C	Thomas Cleaver.....	M	St
John Joyner	I C	I C	John Dunckly	M	St
			William Yorke	M	I

NORTHAMPTON.

	1702	1705		1702	1700
Samuel Hickman	S	St	John Whitethorne	S	I
Alexander Tayler	S		John Dawes..........	I	C
Thomas Webster	S		Hugh Garly..........	I	C
William Robinson	S	St	Francis Reading......	I	C
John Hickman	S	St	Matthew Honor	S	I
John Desborow	S	St	Thomas Stirk	I	C
John Luck	S	St	Edward Milam	St	I
Timothy Rogers......	S	St	Edward Hilliard......	I	C
Richard Newell	S	C	Francis Batten	I	C
Thomas Judkins......	S	St	Nicholas Mason	S	St
Richard Hatt	S	St	William Gooday......	I	C
Richard Gardiner	S	St	Benjamin Bullivant ..	I	C
Thomas Caldicutt, Esq.	S	I	Robert Ives	I	C
John Adkins	S	St	Robert Linwood	I	C
John Lockey	S	C	Robert Sanders	I	C
Robert Chambers	S	St	Samuel Maning	S	St
Nathaniel Weston	S	St	Thomas Brightman....	S	St
Samuel Bateman	S	St	James Green	S	I
William Percival.....	S	St	Edward Battin	I	C
John Packwood	S	St	Theophilus Burditt. ..	I	C
John Luck	S	St	Dr. Shelton..........	I	C
Thomas Leale........	S	I	Thomas Atterbury	I	C
Abraham Hayes.....	S	I	John Carter..........	S St	M St
John Sparrow........	S	St	William Robins	S St	M St
Ferdinand Archer	S	St	Edward Hodgkins	S St	M St
Samuel Clifford	S	I	James Hackleton	St St	M St
William Pettit	S	I	Daniel Singleton.	S	I M St
John Oldham	S	I	James Weston........	S St	M St

Poll books can often provide useful information about your ancestors before civil registration began - this poll book at TheGenealogist.co.uk covers much of 18th century Northants

smaller towns and rural areas and from the mid-19th century the numbers of directories grew tremendously. Directories were usually published annually and were known by the name of their publisher such as Pigot's, White's, Kelly's and Bulmer's. Information in directories could be up to a year out of date by the time they went to print.

Trade directories were initially aimed at commercial travellers who wanted to know more about the place they were visiting and how to get there, as well as who they could sell their products to. Therefore, they frequently give details not just of local tradesmen and residents but of the nature of a town, its industries, the times of the local carrier and

Children Baptized in the year of our Lord — 1815

21 Edward the Son of Evan & Mary Field Nantyllan 8
in the Parish of Llangynfelyn was Baptized Feb the 18 by A S
22 Edward the Son of Richard & Elizabeth Jenkin his wife of
Penbont in the Parish of Llanfihangel was Baptized June the 19 A S
23 John the Son of John & Margaret Loyd of Tanygaer in the
Parish of Llanfihangel was Baptized July the 17 by A S
24 John the Son of Thomas & Chatherine Morgan Brynmawr
in the Parish of Llanbadarn was Baptized Feb 17 by A S
25 Thomas the Son of Thomas Jones & Jane Edward Pentre
Bach in the Parish of Llanfihangel was Baptized Jan'y the 12 A S
Mary the Daughter of
was Baptized January 9th by A Shadrach
Susan the Daughter of Daniel Titus & Rachel his wife of
Buell in the parish of Llanddewy was baptized August 30
Margret the Daughter of Lewis & Elizabeth Edwards of Llanbadarn was baptized Dec 25
Jane the Daughter of John & Jane Morgan of Llanbadarn
was baptized August 7 A S
        the son of Edward & Elizabeth Jones of Dole in the
parish of Llaniangel ejener-glyn was baptized Nov 13
        Son of   of same
in the Parish of Llanbadarn was Baptized Nov 11th
        the son of William & Elizabeth Rowland of Bronny
gwndwn in the parish of Llaniangel was baptized Nov 15
Evan the son of Morris Benjamin & Mary his wife of Party-
in the parish of Llaniangel-gener-glyn was baptized Nov 17
David the son of David & Sophiah Morgan of Toaly bont in
the parish of Llaniangel gone r-glyn was baptized Dec 29
Mary the Daughter of
near the house of William Lewis the parish of
Llanbadarn was baptized Jan 9 A S
David the son of Richard & Elizabeth Hughes of Llanbadarn
was baptized April 21
John the son of John & Margaret Lewis shoomaker of Aberystwyth was
Baptized April the 24 by A S

in 1742 to serve the congregations of the Baptists, Independents and Presbyterians within a 12-mile radius of London, it soon began to be used by members of many nonconformist churches throughout the UK who wished to formally register the births of their children. Some records were recorded several years after the event they related to and the earliest entry is for 1716. The register ends in 1840. Similarly there was also the Wesleyan Methodist Registry (1818-1838) which registered births and baptisms of Wesleyan Methodists throughout England, Wales and elsewhere. These include some retrospective births records dating back to 1773.

Don't presume that because, for example, your 20th century family were strict members of the Church of England, all of their predecessors were too. It is safe to say that the majority of us will have had ancestors who attended nonconformist churches at some point in their lives. If your family were Catholics you will usually need to contact the relevant local Catholic church where the majority of Catholic registers are held.

Among the BMD Registers collection you will also find records of 'clandestine' marriages which took place in the Fleet Prison and the King's Bench Prison. These were marriages which did not conform to the strict regulations relating marriage as laid down by the Church of England. Many were carried out by ministers of religion who were in gaol for debt! Despite this, until 1754, they were still valid marriages and many people chose to be married in this way if their marriage was frowned upon by the family or if they wished to marry in a hurry.

Gravestones and memorial inscriptions

Use to: verify and add to core facts. Help find missing records using the new information you have learned

Period: 17th-21st century

Although not a core source, gravestones can provide vital information in your hunt for your ancestors, including details of dates of birth and death, occupations and even causes of death. They can be crucial if you are having difficulties identifying a death certificate for your ancestor, since the date of death will narrow down the number of possible entries in the death index. The age at death will also help you locate the correct birth or baptism record. They are also important for locating other relatives of whom we may have been unaware, but who feature on the same stone or neighbouring ones.

Historians and enthusiasts have been recording the wording on gravestones for many years and the end product of such churchyard surveys are often known as memorial or monumental inscriptions. Surveys carried out in the 19th century or before are particularly precious since they recorded so many stones which are now illegible as a result of modern-day pollution. Many historical surreys are now available online, while there are also many projects under way to record and photograph those gravestones which are still legible. A good example of a collection of 19th century churchyard surveys are those carried out by Leland Duncan, now available online via the website of the Kent Archaeological Society. Many other surveys can be located by a simple internet search. TheGenealogist runs the International Headstone Image Database, a rapidly growing database of gravestones providing information on where an ancestor is buried as well as details of the wording on the memorial and a photograph.

While it is exciting to visit a churchyard in the hope of seeing a gravestone for your ancestors, many stones do not survive, plus your ancestor may not have been buried in the place you expect if in his later years he moved away to live with his grown up children. Gravestones only became affordable for the majority of the public towards the end of the 19th century so your ancestor's grave may never have been marked by a stone. Even after this date you will still find many people buried in a so-called 'pauper grave' where several people were buried in the same space with no memorial. My great grandmother Mary Wilson died in 1928 and, although the family were once fairly well off, they must have fallen on hard times, for she was buried in such a grave in Whitton

GRAVESTONE: Joseph Bowman

Gravestones can provide a wealth of information about a family. The stone for the Bowman family in Lamplugh churchyard, Cumberland, gives not only dates of death for several family members but effectively draws a mini family tree. We also learn that the family had connections with London, since young John Bowman died there in 1851. Locating his stone in Highgate might provide further details of where the family lived in London. The stone reads:

Joseph Bowman of Hodyoad House and Sarah his wife the former of whom died Jan 22nd 1850 Aged 84 years. The latter died April 16th 1823 Aged 68 years. Sarah their daughter died June 14th 1822 aged AE [aged] 26 years. Agnes the wife of John Bowman their son died Nov 18th 1827 AE 34 years. And Harriet Jane his second wife died April 26th 1833 AE 26 years. Anthony Hamilton the son of Harriet Jane and John Bowman died in London Jany 8th 1850 aged 14 Years and was Interred in Highgate Cemetery. Agnes the daughter of Agnes and John bowman died at Hawkshead May 29th 1851 aged 35 Years.

will know for certain whether or not there was an inquest and whether you need to search for further records. You can also search for your ancestor's death using online newspaper archives such as the British Newspaper Archive since the majority of inquests were reported by local newspapers – but don't rely on this as a complete substitute for buying the certificate, as coverage is far from complete and a small proportion of inquests were not reported in the newspapers.

It's also worth checking the online archives of the national daily newspapers just in case your ancestor's demise was sufficiently newsworthy to feature there. He may for example have died in a disaster such as a shipwreck or rail accident.

Death certificates were only introduced on 1 July 1837 in England and Wales and before the 1850s there were far fewer newspapers carrying local news, so it is harder to determine if a death was subject to an inquest before this period. However, make a thorough sweep of online catalogues for the county record office or offices which cover your ancestors' places of residence. Some have indexed their coroners' records by name of the deceased. Make sure you have located the burials for each of your ancestors and note any death that appears to have occurred before old age. You will also sometimes find comments regarding causes of deaths in burial registers or on gravestones, especially where the death was a violent or tragic one.

Survival rates for inquest records are patchy, while the records are closed to the general public until they are over 75 years old. For these reasons, as mentioned above, it is frequently easier to see if there is a report of the inquest in the local newspaper, either in online collections or at the local library or archives. You may, however, glean further information from any inquest records that do survive, so it is always worth checking these too.

Surviving inquest records from 1752 onwards will usually be held by the record office that covers the area where your ancestor's death took place. Up to 1860 they were filed in with Quarter Sessions records and so you may well need to search through these records for the date you require, if the record office has not indexed them.

Among the Quarter Sessions records you may also find coroner's bills which can be a useful substitute if a full inquest record cannot be found. From 1752 coroners were paid £1 plus expenses for attending an inquest and, although the bills were created purely for the coroner to claim his money, they also provide details of the name of the deceased, place and date of inquest and verdict given. After 1860, although surviving inquest records are not filed with Quarter Sessions records, they will still be held

SEARCH TIP

Unless your surname is a particularly common one, search online catalogues and records using your ancestor's surname alone, not adding their Christian name. You may locate inquest reports for wider family members in this way and, although they may not be your direct ancestor, their death will have had an effect on the family as a whole. In this way I discovered details of the tragic death of Joseph Westwood who was killed by a strike of lightning while out cutting bracken. He was just 21 years old. I also learned that his younger brother Thomas was also struck, although he survived.

at the record office. A good guide to what survives for which area is *Coroners' Records in England and Wales* by Jeremy Gibson and Colin Rogers (3rd edition, The Family History Partnership, 2009). As with any source it is always a good idea to also contact the relevant record office to confirm they do hold what you wish to see before you make your journey, in case the records have been moved or are currently unavailable.

Before 1752 records are held at The National Archives in Kew while those dated before 1733 will usually be in Latin. Take a look at TNA's research guide on coroners' records for further details. Transcriptions of a proportion of inquest records have been published, such as Roy Hunniset's *Sussex Coroners' Inquests 1485-1558* published by Sussex Record Society.

Types of inquest records

Various records were produced as a result of an inquest. These include the actual 'inquisition' itself, which detailed the place and date of death, names of the jury members, the official verdict given as to the cause of death and a brief summary of the circumstances. This would have been accompanied by depositions. These were witness statements given by those who were either present when the deceased died or (in the case where suicide is being considered) those who knew him well or who had seen him shortly before his death. These are the most valuable of records, for they are the ones which will tell you more about your ancestor and often his family too. Here you will frequently learn about his daily routine, the place or exact nature of his employment, his relationships with other family members and the exact circumstances either leading up to his death or the discovery of his body if no one was present when the death occurred. If there was any possibility that your ancestor might have taken his own life then there will also have been questions asked about his financial status and state of mind.

Wills

Use to: confirm a pedigree and find out more about your ancestors' lives and property

Period: 15th-21st centuries

Not all of our ancestors made wills (about one in ten until the 19th century when figures rose), but these records are one of a researcher's most important sources, especially for proving a family tree to pedigree level. They not only confirm who was related to whom but frequently record names and relationships for many different family members all within the one document, helping you to grow your family not just backwards but sideways too. They will also tell you a lot more about your family in terms of where they lived, what they did and what land and other property they owned. Reading their will may even give you an insight into their character. Wills cover a wide range of dates, meaning that you may be lucky enough to find a will which pre-dates parish registers and takes your tree back to the early 1500s; you can also use them to find out more about family members who died in the 20th and 21st centuries.

Although you may find a copy of a will among family papers, the great majority of wills are located using the records of the various probate courts. When someone wrote a will they named one or more people as executors. The role of the executor was to carry out the wishes of the deceased as written in his will. 'Proving a will' is the name given to the process whereby the executors applied to the probate courts for permission to administer the estate of the deceased. If satisfied that the will was in order and the executors were who they claimed to be, the probate court would make a 'grant of probate' and give the executors a written record of this, which they could use in order to close bank accounts and make payments from the deceased's estate. This process remains basically the same today.

From 13 January 1858 all wills in England and Wales were proved by a hierarchy of secular probate courts often known as registries. The Principal Probate Registry headed the probate court system and produced an annual index of all wills proved from 1858 onwards. This is available to search online at **https://probatesearch.service.gov.uk/#wills** and wills can be ordered from this website too. The cost is currently £10 for each will but the index is free to search.

Before 13 January 1858 wills in England and Wales were proved by a hierarchy of church courts whose jurisdictions covered different geographical locations. These courts included the probate courts of the two archbishoprics of York and of Canterbury, which were often referred to as

WILL: Edward Wallman

This is the last Will and Testament of me – Edward Wallman of Swavesey in the County of Cambridge Farmer. I give and bequeath my silver cup and punch ladle to my Son Edward absolutely – I give and bequeath all my silver buttons, silver buckles and one of the two ancient guineas in my possession such guinea to be selected within one year from the day of my death by my Daughter and also half a dozen of my silver tea spoons two silver table spoons and a silver cream pitcher (the larger of the two belonging to me). and also my chiming clock and also my best dining table. and also all the furniture bed and bedding which shall at my decease be in my keeping room and in the bed room over the same unto my Daughter Elizabeth absolutely – I give

- From the outset it is clear that Edward Wallman is well-off because he mentions various silver goods and also 'my best dining table' indicating he has more than one dining table
- He goes on to mention 'all my four children Edward Wallman, Jonas Wallman, Ann Thorp and Elizabeth Wallman'. From this we not only know the married name of his daughter Ann, but later in the will he mentions his grandson 'William Wallman, son of my son John'. This must have been another son who had died by the time Edward wrote his will in 1860
- He also mentions his 'copyhold lands' indicating he held land of the manor. This is a vital clue for the researcher to look in any surviving manorial records, especially court rolls. (See page 78 on manorial records.)
- The final paragraph is the part of the will which gives details of when it was proved and who the executors were. These might be different to those names in the will itself if one or more executor had died before Edward. It also gives the date on which probate was granted and in this case the date of death and a value of the estate for probate purposes. This was recorded as 'Under £100' but up to 1898 this figure did not include the value of any freehold land unless it was leased out.

ON the *Twelfth* ~~ day of *October* ~~ 186*1* the Will *of Edward Wallman late of Swavesey in the County of* ~~ . *Cambridge. Farmer* ~~ ~~

deceased, who died on the *Seventh* . day of *August* 186*1*, at *Swavesey aforesaid* was proved in the District Registry attached to Her Majesty's Court of Probate at *Peterborough* ~~ ————— by the Oaths of *Elizabeth Wallman of Swavesey aforesaid Spinster . the Daughter , Samuel Thorp of the same place Butcher and Farmer and James Vaughan of the Town and County of Huntingdon . Solicitor, the*

Execut*ors* therein named *they* having been first sworn duly to administer.

the Prerogative Courts of Canterbury (PCC) and York (PCY) respectively. The PCC had jurisdiction over all of England south of the River Trent and also over Wales, while the PCY had jurisdiction of England north of the River Trent. Within these regions there were other, less important (and therefore less expensive) probate courts, including archdeaconry courts and diocesan courts (under the authority of the bishop).

There was one further type of probate court known as a 'peculiar'. Peculiar courts did not fall under the jurisdiction of the local archdeacon or bishop for probate purposes, but were in the hands of a separate body entirely – this could be a local vicar, a dean and chapter of a cathedral or a secular authority such as a lord of the manor. The majority of these peculiar jurisdictions originated as favours given by the crown to the particular person or institution, probate fees bringing in a lucrative income.

There were various rules determining which court your ancestor's will could be proved in, but the rule of thumb for researchers is to make sure you have checked all those that had jurisdiction in the area where your ancestor lived or had connections ie where they were likely to have held land or property.

The Prerogative Courts of Canterbury and York levied much higher probate fees and a substantial proportion of the wills proved in these courts related to wealthier estates; however, there is also a significant proportion of wills proved here relating to estates belonging to the less well off, so make sure you check the will indexes of whichever of these covered the area where your ancestor lived. Between 1812 and 1858 anyone holding any Bank of England stocks or shares had to have their will proved in the PCC, while other executors may have chosen to have a will proved in the PCY or PCC because it was more convenient or because they felt it offered more privacy.

You should ensure you have searched all courts where probate could have taken place. This will include all archdeaconry, diocesan, and peculiar courts covering the area where you ancestor lived as well as the PCC or PCY. One of the best guides to determine which courts you should be searching is Jeremy Gibson and Else Churchill's book, *Probate*

INDEXES & CALENDARS

Whether you are searching online or in the record office, you may find yourself looking at either a will index or a will calendar. Whereas an index is an alphabetical listing of testators by name, a calendar is semi-alphabetical, names of testators being grouped according to the initial letter of the surname and then ordered chronologically within that grouping.

INVENTORY: William Reed

Before 1782 there should be an inventory with a will. This inventory goes with the will of William Reed of Huby in Yorkshire, who died in 1730. It gives an excellent idea of the number of rooms in his house and also an insight into life in his household . William was a maltster and a farmer and thus we see items relating to farming and also brewing – a kimlin was a vessel used in the brewing process.

March 3rd 1740. A True Inventory of all the Goods, Chattels and Moveables, belonging to William Reed of Hewby, late Died. Valued by us whose names are under written.

First His purse and Apparell	£10 0s 0d

In the House:

One clock, nine pewter Dishes, one Duzen of Plates, two Tables, six Chairs, Two iron potts, one kettle one pan and other household implements	£4s 6d 0d
One Bed & Bedstead with Bedding thereto belonging one	£4 6 s 6d
Table half a Dozen Chairs with other Implements	

In the Little parlour

One Bedstead with Bedding belonging	
One Chest of Drawers one panell Chest	
One warming pan	
One Table one Seeinglass [mirror] with other Implements	£3 5s 0d

In the Back parlour

One Bed two Bedsteads	£1 10s 0d

In the Meal chamber

One Kimlin with other Hustlements [household goods of little value]	£0 10s 0d

In the Fore Chamber

One Bed and Beeding [bedding] and Bedstead one Chest one press with other Implements	£1 10s 0d

In the Dary [Dairy]

One Barrell Churn, two Dozen Bowls with other wood vessel	£0 13 s 0d
One Kettle in the Furness	£0 12 s 0 d
Six two year old Bease [beasts]	£9 0s 0d
Six three year old Bease	£14 0s 0d
Twenty Sheep	£3 0s 0d
Five year old Calves	£5 0s 0d
Two foles [foals]	£2 0s 0d
Four Young Horses	£12 0s 0d
Two mares	£2 10s 0d
Seven Acres of wheat corn in the Closes	£10 10s 0d
Eight Quarters of Barly	£8 0s 0d
Eight quarter of Ry[e]	£12 16s 0d
Three Quarters of wheat	£6 12 s 0d
Four oxen	£18 0s 0d
Three Mares	£9 0s 0d

Twenty Quarters of Malt	£30 0s 0d
Twenty Quarters of Barly	£28 15s 0d
Two Kines [cattle]	£5 0s 0d
Two Waggons two plows (ploughs) two Harrows and all the rest of Husbandry Geer	£12 0s 0d
Winter Corne in the Fields	£30 0s 0d
Debts in the Book	£50 0s 0d
One Sow and Piggs	£1 10 s 0d
Six Kine	£20 0s 0d
Total	£311 11s 6d

Signed by: William Brown, William Tate, John Bland and Robert Smith (his mark).

Jurisdictions; Where to Look for Wills. (Federation of Family History Societies, 2002). Although it is now out of print you can usually find secondhand copies via websites such as **www.abebooks.co.uk**, and many local libraries have copies. For updates regarding the location of will indexes compiled since the book was published go to **https://community.dur.ac.uk/a.r.millard/genealogy/probate.php**.

Otherwise, look at the website of the county record office which covers the area you are interested in, as many will have uploaded guides to local wills and where to find them.

Wills for the PCC are available via **TheGenealogist.co.uk**, where there is a name index from which you can download images of the wills. It also offers a variety of will indexes for many parts of the country including Irish prerogative court will indexes. PCY wills are held at the Borthwick Institute at the University of York. While many will images and will indexes are online many more have still not been digitised and you may need to visit the relevant county record office to see them.

Inventories

Before 1782 you should also look for the inventory which would have accompanied your ancestor's will. These are usually filed with the will and list the personal goods of the deceased (they do not include real estate), giving each item, or group of items, listed with a monetary value. Inventories were required by the probate courts in order to assess the probate fee.

Inventories are valuable records because they give us an insight into what our ancestor's lives were like, what sort of possessions they owned, their standard of living and, in many cases, also an idea of the nature of their house since goods were often listed on a room-by-room basis.

Letters of administration and death duty records

Even if a person did not write a will you may find letters of administration, especially where there were debts owed by the deceased's estate. In that case a next-of-kin would usually apply to the probate court for letters of administration, which gave them authority to administer the estate. As well as the letters themselves you will also find an administration bond, where the next-of-kin signed a bond promising to make a full inventory of the deceased's estate and pay any debts owed.

If your ancestor died between 1796 and 1903 you may also be able to find their death duty record. Death duties were payable on most estates by 1857. Although the original records are at TNA, those for 1796-1811 relating to all wills apart from those proved in the PCC are available to download from TNA's website. The death duty register will tell you exactly how much was in the estate when the person died, how much tax was paid, who were the main beneficiaries, the names of the executors and also the deceased's date of death. For further information there is an excellent guide to the subject on TNA's website. From 1898 the exact value of the estate would also have been recorded at the foot of the will when probate was granted.

Scotland and Ireland

Scottish wills up to 1901 can be accessed at **www.scotlandspeople.gov.uk**. Ireland had a similar system to the English system of civil probate courts from 1858, headed by the Principal Registry in Dublin. After the partition of Ireland in 1921, a Principal Registry was also formed in Belfast to serve Northern Ireland. However, many original pre-1922 probate records were destroyed in a fire, a devastating loss of this very important source. The calendars of wills and administrations from 1858, held at the National Archives of Ireland (NAI) in Dublin and at Public Record Office for Northern Ireland (PRONI) do survive. Proni has some will calendars online at **www.proni.gov.uk/index/search_the_archives/will_calendars**. For pre-1858 wills, again use the aforementioned Gibson Guide.

Parish chest and workhouse records

Use to: find out more about your ancestors' lives, especially those who were poor; and to trace bastard ancestors

Period: 17th-19th century

You may be able to find out more about your ancestors and their lives by using administrative records created by the parish where he or she lived. From the mid-15th century until the late 19th century, the church was also in charge of secular administration in each parish. The vicar was, therefore, responsible for the maintenance of the parish church and the welfare of his parishioners' souls, but he and his deputies also had responsibility for the maintenance of the local roads, the collection of the poor rate and its distribution, providing for children born out of wedlock and maintaining law and order at a local level. The actual running of the parish was in the hands of the local 'vestry', a committee formed of local parishioners and named this because they originally met in the vestry of the church. Each year the vestry elected a selection of parish officers to undertake certain positions of importance in the parish. These roles were usually unpaid and in many cases unpopular. They included the churchwarden (of which there were usually two but sometimes more in larger parishes), the overseers of the poor, the constable and the waywarden, who was in charge of the highways.

The parish system produced much paperwork and there are several key sources you can look for, although survival rates for each parish do vary greatly. As a group they are sometimes referred to as 'parish chest records' because they were originally stored in a large chest in the church. These days you will find them in county record offices.

Vestry minutes and rate books

Vestry minutes record what was decided at each vestry meeting and who attended. Here you may see your ancestor's signature at the foot of each meeting if he was on the vestry and attended regularly, while you may also see his election to one of the parish offices. Vestry minutes record anything from the mundane every day running of parish, such as the setting of the yearly rates, through to accounts of more notable events that affected villagers or the village as a whole.

You may find rate books relating to church rates, which provided funding for the church and its maintenance, poor rates which provided sufficient funds to give poor relief to the needy poor, and for highway maintenance.

The amount of rates that your ancestor paid was determined by the value of the property he owned or occupied. Rate books record the owner and occupier of a property, describe or name the property eg 'House and garden' and give its acreage, its rental value and its rateable value. All but the poorest of villagers should feature and where a surviving run of rate books survives they can provide a picture of the wealth of successive generations of a family. If one property remained in a family for several generations, the disappearance of one family member from the rate books and the introduction of the name of a new family member who appears to have been assessed for the same property can help prove a pedigree and narrow down the date of death of the earlier ancestor.

Account books

Account books were kept by the various different parish officers, notably the churchwardens, overseers of the poor and constables. You may find your ancestors listed in any of these, perhaps in those of the churchwarden, being paid for work done to repair the church or even for killing local vermin. The churchwardens had a fund out of which parishioners would be paid from bringing them the heads of any type of animal or bird considered to be vermin, ranging from sparrows and crows through to polecats – all of which might destroy crops.

In rare cases, churchwardens' accounts may even pre-date parish registers and in others they make up for missing parish registers. In Kendal (Cumbria), for example, the parish registers are missing between 1632 and 1678. There is a set of churchwardens' accounts from this period and these are good substitutes for the burial register because whenever somebody was buried the fee for the burial service would be recorded together with the name of the person buried.

Look out, too, for constables' account books. One of the many jobs allocated to the parish constable was to escort people to goal to await trial and details of who these were and their offence is often included in these records, where they survive. The constable was also responsible for removing unwanted poor people from the parish and they too may be recorded as he would record his expenses for doing so in the accounts.

Overseers' accounts

Records relating to the poor were the remit of the overseers of the poor. Their account books probably make the most fascinating reading of the three main parish officers (churchwardens, overseers and constables), often providing details regarding poor relief, to whom it was given and its nature, eg whether it was a monetary payment or payment in kind, such as food or clothes. Survival rates for overseers' accounts are good from the early 18th century onwards.

Although your ancestors may have been in regular employment, it only took the premature death or injury of the breadwinner to push them over the dividing line between being self-sufficient and needing poor relief. In the early 1800s, following a series of wars with France and a succession of poor harvests, England was thrown into an extremely bad economic depression and one in 20 sought poor relief on at least one occasion.

Overseers' accounts for 1829 for the parish of Pembury in Kent show that a remarkable number of people were regularly receiving poor relief. Researching families by the name of Sisley and Whiting, there were regular entries along these lines:

- *19 June 1830*   *paid John Sisley no work*   *1s*
- *26 June 1830*   *paid William Sisley no work*   *3s 6d*
- *28 Jun 1830*   *paid William Whiting as allowed for clothes children*   *5s*
- *27 Nov 1830*   *paid John Sisley ill*   *2s*
- *1 Jan 1831*   *paid William Sisley ill*   *4s.*

Where such overseers' records survive, you can often learn far more about your poorer ancestors than many of their middle class equivalents.

Only those people officially 'settled' in a parish were entitled to receive poor relief from parish funds. A person's place of 'settlement' was the parish that had responsibility for him if he required poor relief. Until 1662 settlement was usually based on someone's place of birth, but from this date your ancestor would usually have inherited his or her father's place of settlement, although this could change if he were, for example, apprenticed to someone in a different parish. A woman gained her husband's place of settlement when she married. Assessing who qualified for poor relief and who did not (and should therefore be removed to their correct parish of settlement) produced a significant amount of paperwork and the sources you should look out for include settlement certificates, settlement examinations and removal orders. These records can tell you a lot about your ancestor's family that will not be documented elsewhere.

Settlement records

Until 1759 the overseers could remove someone who did not have settlement in the parish even if they had not sought poor relief. If a person's place of settlement was uncertain the overseers would question the person to try and discern where it was likely to be. Across the country relatively few settlement examinations survive but, where they do, they can provide vital biographical data concerning your ancestor, including his father's place of birth, any employment he had taken, stints in the army and also details of his wife and any dependent children. These records may show that your ancestor had wandered many miles from where he originally came from, providing evidence as to where your family originated. Contentious cases were also heard in the Quarter Sessions courts so it is worthwhile checking their records too. (See page 74.)

From 1662 documents known as settlement certificates could be issued by the overseers in a person's home parish if he wished to travel to another parish to find work. They acted as proof of that person's place of settlement and guaranteed that the parish would take him back and pay him and his family poor relief if he required it. Once the poor person arrived in the new parish he would hand in the certificate to the overseers there, who would store it safely. A copy would also be kept by the home parish so if both copies survive you might find them in your ancestor's parish of origin and the parish he moved to. The certificate gave details of the person's parish of settlement, the parish he intended to move to and of any dependents. You may find full details of children including ages.

If a person was to be removed by the parish overseers back to his home parish, the overseers obtained a removal order from the local Justices of the Peace. This gave similar details to the settlement certificate showing where the person was currently residing, giving details of any dependents and the parish they were to be removed to. Settlement certificates and removal orders are very important documents since they will indicate a person's parish of settlement, which will often be the parish he grew up in and the place where he was baptised. Just because a removal order was issued does not mean the family removed. Illness or childbirth could prevent a removal, or the two parishes concerned might come to an agreement that allowed the family to stay where they were with the home parish paying for their maintenance. This was often the case where it was recognised that poor relief was only required temporarily.

Illegitimacy

At some point in your research you will probably find an ancestor who was illegitimate. In many cases this will be the end of your research into the paternal line as fathers' names are rarely mentioned on birth certificates or in baptism records. If the birth took place before 1834, however, there is a chance you may be able to discover who the father was using parish chest records. Until 1743 illegitimate children took their place of birth as their legal place of settlement and after this date they took their mother's parish of settlement. Whatever the date, the aim of the parish authorities would be to ensure that the child did not become a burden on the parish and the way to do this was to determine who the father was. This led to several different types of records which you can search for. First of all look in the record office catalogue to see if any overseers' accounts survive for that date. Here you may well find maintenance payments naming the child or the mother and the man who had been identified as the father and was making the payments. These would often cover both the mother's confinement and the cost of caring for the child until it was old enough to be apprenticed or go out to work.

You should also check the catalogue to see if there are any surviving bastardy examinations, bastardy bonds or bastardy warrants. The first involved the interrogation of the mother in order to find out who the father was. In many cases, where the birth had already taken place, the midwife would be called in as a witness as it was part of her duty to encourage unmarried mothers to name the man responsible as they were giving birth, this being the time they were most likely to do so! Bastardy examinations may also be found among the Quarter Sessions records and may also give you the date and place of birth of the child, if not always its name, although the latter can usually be deduced from the baptism register.

A bastardy bond legally tied the father to making regular maintenance payments and will provide details of the father's name and the identity of the women who was expecting or had borne his child. In some cases the alleged father would absent himself and in that case a warrant would be issued by the JPs in order to bring him back and face his responsibilities. Again, this will give similar details of the alleged father and whose child he was supposed to have fathered.

With the introduction of union workhouses from 1834 (see overleaf) the rules on bastardy changed and the responsibility for providing for an illegitimate child now shifted to the mother, who found that any

SEARCH TIPS

As already mentioned, survival rates for all those records termed 'parish chest records' vary greatly between parishes. When searching online record office catalogues you will need to search using the different type of record names rather than the general term 'parish chest records'. For example, look for 'settlement certificate' or simply 'settlement' or 'churchwarden' plus the name of the parish. If you are actually in the record office itself many still maintain card indexes listing each record type they hold for a parish. These are far quicker to search, so browse through the cards for each parish of interest.

maintenance claims against putative fathers became much harder to prove. After 1834 you will rarely find bastardy examinations, bonds or warrants, except perhaps in areas of the county where the new union workhouse system took longer to establish.

Apprenticeships

Before 1834, local parish officials would frequently put some effort into arranging an apprenticeship for the child in question once he or she reach the age of about 12 or 14. Many parish officials favoured apprenticing such children to masters in other parishes since an apprentice who served his full term took on his master's place of settlement – thus ridding the original parish of a another potential needy person. Search the CRO catalogue to see if there are any surviving apprenticeship indentures and also check the vestry minutes and overseers' accounts, either of which may mention the arrangement of such apprenticeships. See page 71 for more on apprenticeships.

Workhouse records

In 1834, in an attempt to crack down on the amount of poor relief being paid, the government introduced new legislation affecting poor relief. There were two notable changes as a result of the new legislation. Firstly, poor relief was no longer to be administered by parish officials, but to be organised by 'union'. A union covered approximately a 20-mile radius and included several parishes. It was headed locally by a group of men (and later women too) known as Guardians of the Poor, who were elected annually from the ratepayers of each parish in the union. They were aided by relieving officers who dealt with applications for poor relief and who gradually replaced the overseers of the poor.

The second major difference was the fact that poor relief was no longer given in the form of money or clothes or food. Any one requiring poor relief had to enter the workhouse and the idea behind this was to discourage people from claiming poor relief. Once inside families were split up and life was harsh.

A variety of workhouse records may survive for you to search. The best place to look for listings of which records survive for each workhouse, as well as information on workhouse life and a history of each house and the poor law is Peter Higginbotham's website at **www.workhouses.org.uk**. The larger the workhouse, the greater variety of records you are likely to find, although not all will survive. Most records will be housed in the local record office and the Higginbotham website will tell you which repository holds them.

As is the case with many sources, you may not know whether or not your ancestor features in them before you look. Even if you feel that your family was unlikely to have entered the workhouse at any time because they were not poor enough, bear in mind that temporary unemployment, perhaps caused by illness or injury, could be enough to force a family that had always managed without relief until then into the workhouse, while many older people who were unable to work any longer might end up in the workhouse towards the end of their lives, or if they became ill. By the later part of the 19th century many workhouses became places of care for the sick, while some even had separate hospital wings. By the end of the 19th century workhouses were also the place where many unmarried mothers gave birth. Check any surviving registers of births and baptisms as well as admissions records.

A good place to start is to search for creed registers. These were kept by the larger workhouses and, since they are arranged semi-alphabetically by initial of a person's surname, they are quicker to search than admission and discharge register, which are recorded chronologically. If your ancestor died in the workhouse they will not just be listed in any surviving registers of deaths but also in the discharge registers. A few workhouses also had their own burial grounds.

Military records

Use to: find about ancestors who served in the armed forces

Period: 16th to 20th century

Whether you are searching for a relative who served in World War One or an ancestor who was in the regular army, navy or served in the militia (a part-time force organised within each county) there are many records waiting for you. Here are a few to get you started, but you can read more about this massive subject using TNA's military and maritime research guides **www.nationalarchives.gov.uk/help-with-your-research/research-guides**

Many of our ancestors would have served during one of the world wars. Records for WW2 are not available on general access at present, but if you are the next-of-kin of someone who served, you can apply for their service records from the Ministry of Defence's website at **www.gov.uk/get-copy-military-service-records/overview**. These will give you the bare bones of their service but don't expect to get a lot of detail. If an ancestor died in WW2, his details will be found on the Commonwealth War Graves Website (**www.cwgc.org**) along with all those who died during WW1.

Unfortunately, approximately 60% of WW1 service records were destroyed during bombing in the 1940s. Those which do survive will supply you with plenty of detail about your ancestor, including where he served and personal details such as date and place of birth and next-of-kin. Dates of birth may not be completely accurate as many boys altered their ages in order to join up under age. However, more often than not, there will be no surviving service record, so you will have to rely on other sources.

Check the medal index cards at TheGenealogist or TNA's website, which provide an index of campaign medals awarded to officers and other ranks in the army (including the Royal Flying Corps and the Womens' Auxiliary Army Corps). The index records the name, rank and regimental number and details of the medals awarded. These details can help you identify your ancestor in other records, although, since many men were recorded under their initials rather than full Christian names, it may be hard to identify which entry relates to your ancestor. The original medal rolls, as opposed to the index, are held at TNA (WO 329) and may provide the soldier's battalion number. If you know a man's battalion you can read more about what his battalion got up to on a daily basis using war diaries (WO 95) at TNA, many of which are now available to download for free from TNA's website.

Campaign medals awarded to those who served in the Royal Navy – including the Royal Naval Air Service (RNAS), the Royal Naval Reserve (RNR), the Royal Naval Volunteer Reserve (RNVR) and the Womens' Royal Naval Service (WRNS) – are not online but can be found at TNA in series ADM 171. To help you interpret the abbreviations on the medal cards there is a guide at **www.1914-1918.net/soldiers/interpretmic.html**.

Death certificates can be purchased for all those who died on active service during both world wars, although don't expect full details of the cause of death. The cause of death may simply be given as 'killed in action' or similar. Use the WW1 and WW2 deaths datasets at **TheGenealogist.co.uk** to locate the entry you want and then use the link provided on the accompanying transcription for each entry to order your certificate directly from the government's certificate ordering website run by the GRO/Identity and Passport Service. You can also look for any men who died or were wounded in the casualty lists, which were produced by HMSO on a weekly basis and also published in the *Times, Irish Times* and the *Scotsman*. These were the lists that your families would have studied anxiously each week to see if any loved ones were mentioned. They give details of all those wounded, those who died and those who died after being wounded. They will give the man's surname, initials and his regiment. You can find these at TheGenealogist, while listings of gallantry awards, citations and promotions (for any period) can be found at **www.thegazette.co.uk**, the free website giving access to historical copies of the *London, Edinburgh* and *Belfast Gazettes* respectively.

You may also wish to locate the war memorial where your ancestor is remembered. You can use The Genealogist's growing list of UK war memorials, which also provides a photograph of the memorial and of the location, to help you locate the site. There is a clever system on all of TheGenealogist's WW1 databases which links into the CWGC site so that you can click through to view the results for your ancestor on the CWGC site too. This will list all those commemorated on war memorials abroad as well, and frequently provides details of next-of-kin. A further source is the Prisoner of War records for both WW1 and WW2 at TheGenealogist which are a combination of publications from War Office casualty lists and official lists of British officer prisoners of war.

'Soldiers Who Died in the Great War' is a database of men who died in WW1 and was originally published in 1921. This recorded various details for each soldier and usually includes his regiment or corps, service number, battalion, rank, date of birth, address, where he enlisted, the theatre of war in which he served, his date of death and how he died. Although this is an important database, do check information in other sources where possible as 'Soldiers Who Died' is known for its many inaccuracies, caused by failure to check information at source!

For ancestors who served in the army before WW1, the best starting point are service papers (WO 97) which are searchable by name via TNA's Discovery catalogue. If your search is successful this should give your ancestor's regiment, which will help identify him in other regimental records, such as muster and pay lists which are also held at TNA. See TNA's research guide British Army and Militia 1760-1915.

Royal and merchant navy

If your ancestor was an officer in the Royal Navy, officers' service records (ADM 196) can be located and downloaded using TNA's Discovery catalogue. These cover those who enlisted between 1756 and 1931. Naval Ratings Service records at TNA can similarly be downloaded for those who enlisted between 1853 and 1923 (ADM 139 and 188) and also for those who enlisted before 1923, but served after 1924 (ADM 362 363). For those that joined after 1926, service records are still at the MoD. Until 1861 those serving on board ship were not recorded on census returns. If your ancestor was an officer then you can also look at annual Navy Lists which will give details of promotions and stations for each year. Many of these are available online at TheGenealogist and at TNA. Merchant Navy records are also held at TNA including registers of merchant seaman, crew lists and indexes of boys apprenticed into the merchant navy. There are several useful research guides on the TNA website providing further details.

Business and occupational records

Use to: find about your ancestor's career

Period: guild records can date back to medieval times; business records are most common from the 18th century onwards

There are many ways in which you can find out more about your ancestor's business of career. Depending on his occupation and the date, you may be able to find details of his training and qualifications or notices relating to the running of his business.

To trade in a town or city until about 1850 your ancestor would have been required to be a member of a guild and in many cases also a freeman of the city. Guilds (known as livery companies in London) were associations of merchants or craftsmen originally formed to protect the rights of local tradesman, but over the years they, in fact, developed into powerful authorities within the town of city. In larger towns there were often several guilds relating to the different trades practised there, but in smaller towns there may have just been one guild which covered all trades.

Up to 1750, in order to become a member of a guild your ancestor would have served an apprenticeship to a guild member who ran his own business – he would be known as a 'master' of his trade. Apprenticeships were the provision of training for a boy or girl in return for labour, following a contract being made by both parties and the parents on the child's behalf. The contract (usually called an 'indenture') would be signed and the parents would often make a payment to the master for the child's board and lodging. Most apprenticeships began about the age of 14 and lasted seven years and occasionally the actual indentures survive. They may have been passed down the family or deposited in record offices. If the apprentice completed the period of training success-fully they would then be admitted to the guild, initially working as a journeyman for another guild member. The term 'journeyman' evolved from the French word 'journee' indicating they were paid on a daily basis. Later the journeyman might become a master craftsman himself, employing others and taking on apprentices in his turn. In many cities your ancestor would also have had to apply to become a freeman of the city in order to trade there.

From the 1750s it was possible to join a guild by other means; notably if your father was a member (through patrimony), through buying your way in (by purchase) or in some guilds if your wife's father was a member (through matrimony). From this time on many people began to join guilds which did not necessarily relate to their own trades.

The records created by the system of apprenticeships and guilds and becoming a freeman of a city can not only tell us more about an ancestor's livelihood, but also provide the missing piece of evidence which will show where your ancestor originally came from. Many young boys from rural areas travelled many miles to distant towns or cities in order to take up an apprenticeship. Many settled there after they completed their apprenticeships and, for you as a researcher, this may mean that you have problems finding his baptism. Before the advent of the 19th century census returns and BMD certificates there is often no easy way of linking your ancestor back to the place where he was born and baptised.

A good starting place for apprenticeship records is the records of stamp duty levied on all apprenticeships (exceptions being those arranged for paupers by parish officials and apprenticeships in Ireland). These cover 1710 - 1811. They are available on **TheGenealogist.co.uk** will give the following details:

- names, addresses and trades of the masters
- names of the apprentices and dates of their indentures
- until 1752, name of apprentice's father and place of residence
- amount of stamp duty levied. The rate was 6d for every £1 under £50 which the master received for taking on the apprentice, and 1s for every £1 above £50.

The entry for John Russell in 1732 (below), for example, tells us that, although he was taken on as an apprentice by George Williamhurst, a cooper trading in the City of London, John came from Maidstone in Kent and was the son of William Russell. Unfortunately, after 1752 fewer details are given and from that date it is rare to find details of where the apprentice hailed from. There are also registers of apprenticeships kept by the individual guilds themselves. Many of these have been deposited at county record offices, as have registers of men admitted to the guild itself or to the freedom of the city. These will tell you the date of admission, the person's trade and how he gained admittance – whether through apprenticeship, patrimony or purchase. If it was through patrimony or matrimony you will usually see details of his father or wife too which can be very useful. TheGenealogist has a good collection of freeman's rolls and many of these also provide a useful background to the history of the guilds in the relevant city too.

Use apprentice, guild and freeman's registers or rolls together to potentially trace your ancestor from the point when he started his career, through to becoming a freeman and taking on apprentices himself. You can get an idea of the size of his business by the number of boys he took on.

To find out more about your ancestors in trade from the 1800s onwards you can also use trade directories (see page 32). Look in local newspapers from the 1850s to find notices they may have placed to advertise their business. These will often give full details of what they sold or the services they offered, giving you a good idea of what their business involved. You may also find an auction notice advertising the business for sale. The Gazettes (see page 51) may bring forth notices relating to bankruptcies or dissolutions of business partnerships.

TheGenealogist also has special collections relating to particular occupations, which include railway workers, pilots, actors, lawyers, sports people, doctors and ship's crew lists for naval and merchant navy men. The occupational search section also automatically searches the site's databases relating to biographies, which in turn include various copies of *Who's Who*.

Court records

Use to: learn interesting details of your ancestors' lives (not just for criminals)

Period: Quarter Sessions (England, Wales, and Ireland) from 15th century to 1972; Scotland 1661-1975

Our ancestors did not necessarily have to be criminals to feature in the various different types of court records that are available to the researcher. The court records they are most likely to feature in are those of Quarter Sessions courts, which were found throughout England, Wales and Ireland, with a similar system in Scotland. As the name implies the Quarter Sessions sat four times a year and under the jurisdiction of Justices of the Peace.

Sittings of the Quarter Sessions might last for several weeks or longer and cases were frequently held over to the next sitting. They dealt not just with criminal cases but a great variety of administrative matters. Their records cover a plethora of different matters, some relating to sources which family historians now regard as independent sources eg land, window and hearth tax, and coroners' inquest records. When trying a criminal case a jury would sit alongside the JP.

The important thing to remember is that the great majority of records originally created by, or filed at, the Quarter Sessions will now be held at county or local record offices. Although original Quarter Sessions records can be difficult for researchers to use, especially before 1733 when they were in Latin, most have been well catalogued and many are now searchable by name of those involved via the online catalogue of local record offices and at TNA's Discovery catalogue. Many record offices also hold typed summaries of Quarter and Petty Sessions cases, which make fascinating reading. Some have also been published in book form and many of these can be found at the British Library in London. Jeremy Gibson has produced a guide to surviving records entitled *Quarter Sessions Record for Family Historians* (5th edition, The Family History Partnership). Some Quarter Session records are now online, such as the calendars for Worcestershire Quarter Sessions 1591-1643 at TheGenealogist, while the National Records of Scotland has also digitised a proportion of its Quarter Sessions records. Local newspapers usually carry a roundup of criminal cases from the Quarter and Petty Sessions from approximately 1850 onwards.

Criminal cases heard by the Quarter Sessions typically included cases of theft, assault and vagrancy, while civil matters often related to the levying fines on individuals or parishes who failed to maintain highways or bridges satisfactory, on tradesmen who used incorrect weights, those who failed to attend church, the issuing of licences to innkeepers and gamekeepers, as well as the administration of the local gaols.

Petty Sessions courts were held regularly in between sittings of the Quarter Sessions and helped clear up the overflow of work from the former, issuing licences and dealing with less serious criminal cases which could be tried with a JP alone sitting without a jury.

Quarter Session Courts were superseded by Crown Courts in 1972 following a trial of the latter from 1956 in Liverpool and Manchester.

Assizes

More serious criminal offences were generally held at the assizes. These courts were organised in circuits with judges periodically moving around to different locations within each circuit to hear cases. There were six circuits, known as Home, Western, Oxford, Norfolk, Midland and Northern. Assizes records are held at TNA although not all survive and the assizes did not operate in all regions. Middlesex and the City of London had their own court, the Old Bailey, until 1834 and many records for this can be found online at **www.oldbaileyonline.org**. Bristol and the Palatinates of Cheshire, Durham and Lancashire also had their own courts and their records are held locally. Wales was served by the Court of Grand Sessions of Wales and records are at the National Library of Wales. From 1830 Wales joined the English assize circuit system and records will be at The National Archives.

To find an ancestor whom you suspect was committed for trial in the 19th century, look at HO27, which is online at **TheGenealogist.co.uk** (original records at TNA). This is the Home Office Register of Criminals for England and Wales and gives details of the court of trial, the offence and sentence or a note that he was acquitted. HO 26 (at TNA) covers London and Middlesex 1749-1849 but these counties were included in HO 27 from 1850. TheGenealogist also has Home Office Criminal Entry

THE PALATINATES

The Palatines or Palatinates of Lancaster, Durham and Cheshire were areas which had autonomy from the rest of the country in terms of justice and administration. Historically they had evolved in parts of the country which were difficult to rule from London, and authority to rule would be given to someone the king trusted. For example, the Palatinate of Lancaster arose after the quashing of a rebellion by a group of northern barons. In 1262 King Edward gave authority to his son Edmund, who became the Earl of Lancaster in 1267.

TYPES OF COURT RECORDS

• Depositions: written witness statements and one of the most important sources for finding out more about a case
• Crown minute, gaol and agenda books: list the accused and give summary of case, often noting the plea, verdict and sentence
• Bills of indictment: formal written accusation of the crime. They will give the accused's name and a description of him plus his place of residence, the offence and its date, and name of any victim. The accused's plea, the verdict and sentence might be added after the trail
• Recognizance: an undertaking before the court agreeing to undertake something. This might, for example, be agreeing to behave properly.
Also take a look at TNA's research guide on Criminal Trials in the Assize Courts 1579-1971.

Books (HO 13) which detail letters, warrants and pardons connected with a case and depositions from the Central Criminal Court. These are witness statements used in evidence in trials at the Old Bailey and provide much detail from a case.

You may find your 19th century criminal ancestor was sent to prison in quite another part of the country to that in which he lived, since goals were overcrowded and prisoners were sent to a prison where there was space available. It's worth checking records for HO 23 and 24 as well as the above mentioned sources. These list returns for prisoners in goal throughout England, Wales and Scotland. As well as details of the offence you will also find some descriptions of prisoners' ages and the court of trial.

Transportation

Between the late 16th century and 19th century transportation was seen as a humane alternative to the death sentence and also a solution to the persistent problem of overcrowded goals. Transportees were initially sent to America, but with the outbreak of the American War of Independence this was no longer an option and from 1787 they were sent to Australia instead. Very few convicts were transported after 1857 and the process was formally ended in 1868.

If a family member was transported, a good starting point is the convict transportation registers housed at TNA (HO 11) which cover 1787-1870 and are online as indexed images and transcriptions at **Thegenealogist.co.uk**. These record those convicts transported to Australia between these dates, giving their place of trial, years sentenced, name of ship they were transported on and date of departure from the UK. If your ancestor was sent to New South Wales or Tasmania look at HO 10, listings of convicts settled there between 1787 and 1859 – these can also be found at TheGenealogist These give details of names, ages, where they were living, employment, any cattle or land they owned and sometimes other information too. If your ancestor was transported from Ireland to Australia the National Archives of Ireland holds many records that may list your ancestor and an online database. Go to **www.nationalarchives.ie** and select its 'Genealogy Records'.

Ecclesiastical courts and presentments

As well as civil and criminal courts there were ecclesiastical courts. We have already seen that these dealt with probate matters before 1858, but for centuries they also dealt with 'moral misdemeanours' such as adultery, fornication, blasphemy, defamation, working on a Sunday, not attending church and many more. It was the role of the local churchwarden to put forward ('present') to the court those who were deemed guilty of such offences. The courts were peripatetic and visited each neighbourhood once or twice a year. Anyone found guilty could expect punishments ranging from a fine to excommunication.

Records known as 'presentments', will give details of those presented at court and their offence. These records are held in local record offices and may range in date from the 1600s through to the 1800s. They were suspended during the Civil War, and although they were reinstated after the restoration of the monarchy in 1660, they never regained their former power. By the 19th century most of their authority was removed and the business given to secular courts.

Manorial records

Use to: find out more about your everyday ancestors and possibly to help prove your tree to pedigree level
Period: 13th-20th centuries

Manorial records have a massive potential date range from the 13th century right through to 1922 when the Law of Property Act abolished the last form of land tenure associated with the manorial system known as copyhold land.

Although survival rates are extremely patchy and you may find that few are available for your area of interest, where the manorial court rolls or court books do survive they can be a vital source for proving your family tree to pedigree level.

Early manorial records can be difficult to read before the early 1700s, since they are usually in highly abbreviated Latin, but from this time onwards they are much easier to cope with, and a proportion of manorial records has been transcribed and published. TheGenealogist, for example, has court rolls in book form for both Tooting Bec manor and the manor of Hornsey, while copies of similar volumes for other manors can often be found in secondhand books shops or as digital downloads from websites such as Google Books or the Internet Archive at **www.archive.org**.

There are many different types of manorial records, including court rolls, leases, rentals, surveys and you may even find unproved wills which (because they were unproved) will not be found among the usual probate records.

THE MANORIAL SYSTEM

A manor was an administrative land unit under the charge of a 'lord of the manor'. The lord might be a very wealthy man who held thousands of acres of land and many manors or, by contrast, he might just hold one small manor. Do not confuse a lord of the manor with a 'lord' who sat in the House of Lords and do not presume that the lord would have necessarily have been of noble birth. The manorial system developed under King William I who deemed that all land was the property of the king, and granted it to his vassals in return for the provision of military service and fealty.

After the mid-13th century the need for heavily armed knights and infantry was greatly reduced, so military service was replaced by a payment known as scutage. Alternatively a manor could be held by an ecclesiastical lord who provided the king with ecclesiastical services in return for the land.

While the lords of the manor held their land from the king, they in turn granted parts of their lands to their own tenants, who initially paid for these tenancies by labouring on the lord's land. The lord offered them justice and protection in return. Money payments were gradually substituted for labour services.

The most important type of record for family historians are the court rolls or court books. Many people living on the manor held land from the lord. This meant that he had the right to work and live on that piece of land or cottage. After his death, his next of kin (his heir) was usually entitled to be admitted to the same holding, after the payment of an admission fine (a heriot) and the admission of the new heir would be recorded in the court roll or court book. This is important because details of how the heir was related to the previous land holder are recorded and sometimes in great detail. Thus you may see details of land being passed from father to son or daughter or in a more convoluted fashion via an aunt or uncle or grandparent. There also may be details of second marriages especially if land has been held by a woman.

Where such mini written pedigrees survive, they may be the second piece of evidence (usually along with a baptism entry) which proves an ancestor's parentage to pedigree level. In some cases, where the parish registers do not survive or are extremely lacking in detail, they may be the only piece of firm evidence establishing who was the son or daughter of whom. If you find a successive run of court rolls you may be able to trace your family in this manner over several generations.

Although many manorial records are held at local record offices, some remain with the lord or his successor, while others are held at TNA and other repositories. Use the Manorial Documents Register (MDR) at TNA for a full overview of all known surviving manorial records and their current location. Part of the MDR is now online at **http://apps. nationalarchives.gov.uk/mdr/**.

School records

Use to: find out when and where your ancestor went to school

Period: 16th-20th century

General school education for the working and middle classes evolved in the 19th century under the auspices of the church. In 1798 The British and Foreign School Society (often referred to as The Foreign Society) was founded by the Quaker Joseph Lancaster, and began to establish schools in many parts of the country to which pupils of any religious denomination could come. Although most schools initially concentrated on teaching the Bible, reading and writing, gradually the school curriculum evolved to include other subjects as well. In 1811 the Church of England founded The National Society in direct competition to the Foreign Society. Between them the two societies established a great number of schools around the country.

In 1870 the government passed a new Education Act and this led to the introduction of 'board schools' in areas where it was felt that there were insufficient school places for the number of children. Board schools were funded by government grants and run by a school board consisting of a group of locally elected people. A similar scheme was introduced in Scotland two years later.

Collectively these church and board schools are referred to as 'elementary' schools and many were the forerunners to the primary schools of the 20th century. School attendance was not made compulsory until 1880, however, when children were supposed to attend school until the age of ten years. It was very hard to enforce school attendance and there are numerous cases where families could just not afford the fees (often a penny a week) to send a child to school. In the summer many children remained essential workers for gathering in the harvest and would not attend at these times.

Survival rates for both church and board school records are generally good and include log books, admission registers and punishments books. Some records are still be held by the schools themselves, but many have been deposited in local archives, although records containing entries under 100 years old are not available to the public for privacy reasons.

Admission registers most commonly date from 1880 but can sometimes be found as early as 1862. They will include details of the date the child was admitted, details such as date of birth, next of kin and address and sometimes notes regarding previous schools, when the child left the school and why, or details of what job they took up on leaving.

School log books were maintained by the head teacher and relate to the running of the school. Head teachers were obliged to keep them from 1863 onwards but earlier log books do exist for some schools. The books give a wonderful insight into school life, how the school was run and problems faced by the head teacher, but also include references to incidents concerning staff and pupils.

You may also find punishment books, which list pupils punished and the reason for the punishment, although the latter can be frustratingly vague such as, for example, 'impudence'.

Public school records

Apart from the elementary schools there were also many public schools. Although generally regarded as the remit of the wealthy, many accepted not just fee-paying pupils, but also poorer pupils who received a scholarship, or whose fees were paid by a private benefactor. My ancestor James Wilson attended Sedbergh School in Yorkshire, probably thanks to a private benefactor, since the family could not have afforded the fees. Public school records include school admissions and collections of diaries and letters too. Many public school records have been published and these are often list who attended the school as well as giving biographical notes on pupils' childhood, school years and later careers.

Some entries are longer than others. James Wilson's entry tells me that he was 15 when he joined the school in February 1840, that he left in June the same year and that he was born in Gleaston in Lancashire.

By contrast, the entry for my relative Reginald Remington (below), who went on to become a vicar, has a much longer entry, telling me his name, full date of birth plus full details of all schools and colleges he attended and his address when the book was published! Many schools have their own private archive which the school archivist will usually be happy to search on your behalf. However, many school and university records have been published and a very good collection of these is available at **TheGenealogist.co.uk**.

Remington, Reginald, entered August, age 12; born July 3rd, 1827, at Ulverston; left December, 1842. Afterwards at Macclesfield Grammar School. Pembroke Coll., Oxford, B.A., 1855. Curate of Foxearth, Essex, 1856–1859; of Middleham, Lancashire, 1859–1860; of Downham, 1860–1864; of Holy Trinity, Southport, 1864–1865. Vicar of Fritwell, Oxfordshire, 1876–1882; of Wormsley, Herefordshire, 1889–1890; of Barlings, Lincoln, 1890. Present address :—Barlings Vicarage, Lincoln.

If your ancestor was a teacher in the early 20th century then he or she may feature in the list of teachers registered by the Teachers' Registration Council which began in 1914. The list for 1917 is available at TheGenealogist and will provide you with an address for each teacher which usually represents the school they were teaching at. This may lead you on to find out more via school log books or other administrative records for that school at the local record office.

What to do if you or your ancestor were adopted

There was no formal adoption process In England and Wales before 1927 and so there are unlikely to be any records relating to 'adoption' or fostering of children before this. The system of adoption put in place in 1927 was organised in such a way that it was impossible for anyone giving up a child (or anyone else for that matter) to find him or her under their new identity.

Thegenealogist.co.uk provides an adoption look-up service in the Adopted Children's Register, which has been maintained by the General Register Office since 1927. These give details of the child's adoptive name and date of birth and adoptive parents. These will not, however, link back to the original birth certificate. If you yourself were adopted you can contact the GRO and ask for access to your original birth entry, which will record at least the birth mother's name and address and, in a few cases, that of the birth father.

The GRO also maintains the Adoption Contact Register which is a linking mechanism whereby both adoptees and their blood relatives can place their details on a register. If both child and a blood family member registers, they can then be put in touch. For further information on accessing adoption records go to **www.direct.gov.uk/gro**.

Although you may suspect an ancestor was informally adopted or fostered by another family before 1927, it may be hard to find any proof of this. Family legend may state that such and such an ancestor was given away and you may find that when you hunt for his birth there is no record. While this confirms the likelihood that the family tale is true, it will be impossible to link him back to his original birth family and birth entry unless you know his original birth name or have other clues passed down through the family. Many children who were informally adopted would take on the surname of the new family, although some may have kept their original surname as a middle name or used it sporadically.